MATH ADVENTURES

Grade 2

EDITED BY LINDA BERTOLA

ILLUSTRATIONS BY AGNESE BARUZZI

FlashKids

New York

NOTE TO PARENTS

YOUNG CHILDREN LEARN MATH BEST
IF THEY HAVE FUN WHILE THEY ARE DOING IT!

This book series approaches math as an experience that should be playful and relatable. The stories and activities engage children and invite them to explore the world of numbers. This approach fosters a positive attitude about math and motivates children to keep trying and keep turning pages.

Research shows that children retain knowledge best when they take pleasure in learning. This book is designed to help children find pleasure in learning math.

This book offers a unique blend of storytelling, logic games, and math concepts. Each section begins with a fun story to spark your child's curiosity. The setting and characters are a springboard for the math and logic activities that follow. An endearing owl character guides children through the stories and activities. All the creatures are imaginative, but the situations and tasks (like counting crayons or adding money), are familiar and rooted in daily life.

This book does not emphasize formal math definitions or terminology. Instead, math concepts are introduced gradually and naturally, as part of the story-based framework. To reinforce concepts, suggestions for simple extension activities using common household items are also included.

Children of different ages and math abilities can enjoy this book equally. They can engage with the material on many levels as they explore, discover, and expand their understanding of math.

THIS BOOK
IS AIMED
AT CHILDREN
IN GRADE 2.

Skills and concepts covered:

- Comparing quantities between 10 and 20.
- Grouping by ten.
- Counting up to 100.
- Adding and subtracting.
- Multiplying using repeated addition.
- Performing mental math.
- Solving logic puzzles and games.

Some tips for adults

- Respect children's time and attention span.
If they close the book or skip a page, it does not mean they are giving up. Perhaps they just need to step away and revisit the material later.

- Ask questions instead of giving answers.
When children need help, pose questions to guide them to the problem or mistake.

- Let children set the pace, even if it seems slow or inefficient.
Later, you can always help them discover faster ways to solve a problem.

- Encourage children to think through problems before they begin solving.
Invite children to brainstorm by visualizing, discussing, drawing, or manipulating objects.

- Ask, "How did you do it?"
Invite children to explain their process. It is better for them to grasp the reasoning and logic behind a solution than to just memorize rules.

- Apply math to everyday life.
Help children discover numbers in the world around them. Point out how and when math is used for many daily activities.

CELEBRATE ACHIEVEMENTS BY LETTING
YOUR CHILD PUT A MEDAL STICKER
AT THE END OF EVERY CHAPTER
AFTER COMPLETING IT.

WELCOME TO WOODLAND TOWN

Nestled deep in the mountains, where the winter sun
is too lazy to rise, is Woodland Town. Hidden by dense forest,
this little village has small cottages, big houses, a school,
a tempting pastry shop, a general store, and even a hotel.

From squirrels to snails, forest animals of every size and color
call this village home. Hedgehogs, woodpeckers, ants, and
rabbits live and work side by side. Life is slow, but it's not
always simple. In fact, an unexpected mess can happen
at any moment.

Yesterday, for example, Mouse was awoken by the screams
of Mr. Rabbit . . . who had been pricked by the quills
of Porcupine . . . who had been watching the clouds instead
of where he was going. The forest is full of mischief.

Thankfully, the willing and wise bees soothed poor
Mr. Rabbit with their special ointment.
Quiet fell upon the forest once again, but not for long.
Adventure is always lurking behind a bush or under an anthill.
Turn the page to join these charming creatures on a journey
through Woodland Town.

HELLO! I AM **OWL** AND I WILL BE YOUR
GUIDE THROUGH WOODLAND TOWN.

I KNOW EVERY TREE AND PINE CONE
IN THIS FOREST. JUST FOLLOW ME!

CONNECT THE DOTS FROM 1 TO 16.
COLOR ME IN, AND THEN YOU'RE
READY TO START YOUR JOURNEY!

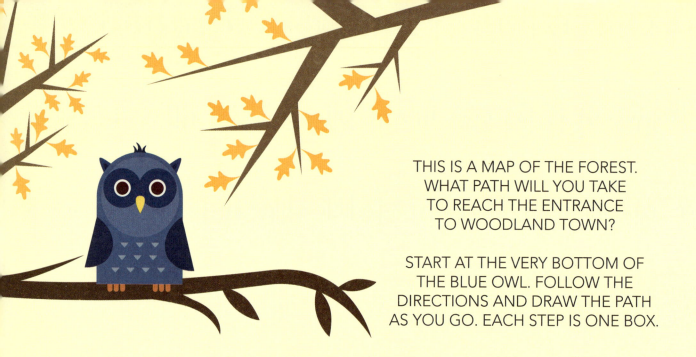

THIS IS A MAP OF THE FOREST.
WHAT PATH WILL YOU TAKE
TO REACH THE ENTRANCE
TO WOODLAND TOWN?

START AT THE VERY BOTTOM OF
THE BLUE OWL. FOLLOW THE
DIRECTIONS AND DRAW THE PATH
AS YOU GO. EACH STEP IS ONE BOX.

Go 3 steps down and stop
at the tip of the old pine tree.
Then take 2 steps to the right.
You are now at the edge of the pond.
Don't get wet!

Continue 5 steps up and stop. You don't want to get
caught in the thorns of the blackberry bush,
so take 2 steps to the right. Phew!

Take two steps straight up,
then 2 more steps to the right.

Now travel 10 steps all the way down.

You made it through the pine grove!
Just take 1 final step to the right.
You have arrived. Great job!

WELCOME TO
WOODLAND TOWN

**YOU HAVE REACHED
OUR VILLAGE.**
WE HAVE HOUSES, TREES, FLOWERS,
ANIMALS . . . AND HIDDEN
NUMBERS! FIND THE **NUMBERS
FROM 0 TO 9** AND CIRCLE THEM.

COUNT THE NUMBER OF FLOWERS, HOUSES, TREES, MUSHROOMS, AND BIRDS IN THE PICTURE. COLOR THE CIRCLES NEXT TO EACH PICTURE TO SHOW HOW MANY YOU FOUND. THEN **WRITE THE TOTAL AMOUNT** IN THE BOXES.

FIND THE **NUMBER** THAT
MATCHES EACH WORD.
DRAW A LINE TO CONNECT
EACH LEAF WITH THE
CORRECT FRUIT.

SIX

FIVE

THREE

EIGHT

SEVEN

3

4

2

TWO

0

1

9

7

6

5

8

ZERO

FOUR

NINE

ONE

THE SNAIL SISTERS HAVE GATHERED PLENTY OF FRUIT. FOLLOW THE DIRECTIONS AND **COLOR THE PIECES OF FRUIT IN EACH BASKET**.

ALL MY PEARS ARE YELLOW.

I HAVE 3 RED APPLES AND 2 GREEN APPLES.

I HAVE 1 GREEN PLUM AND 3 YELLOW ONES. THE REST ARE PURPLE.

CIRCLE THE SNAIL THAT COLLECTED THE MOST PIECES OF FRUIT. **THEN ANSWER** THE QUESTIONS BELOW.

HOW MANY PIECES OF GREEN FRUIT ARE THERE ALTOGETHER?

HOW MANY PIECES OF FRUIT ARE NOT YELLOW?

HOW MANY PIECES OF FRUIT HAVE THEY COLLECTED ALTOGETHER?

11

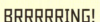

BRRRRRING!

The school bell echoes through the forest at eight o' clock sharp.

Even in the woods, little ones go to class.

Mr. Badger O' Badge is Woodland Town's school teacher.
With his glasses balanced on the tip of his nose, he shares
his woodsy wisdom with young animals.
Every day they learn something new about living in the woods.
Which mushrooms are good to eat?
Where does the sweetest gooseberry grow?
Why does the sky sometimes turn red in the evening?

Mr. Badger O' Badge has an answer for every question.
He gives swimming lessons to land animals, and he teaches
bunnies about bird calls.

BUT MR. BADGER'S FAVORITE SUBJECT IS MATH.

What does math have to do with forest animals? Everything!
Squirrels must count the weeks until winter and add up their
nuts and berries. Woodpeckers must know geometry so they
can hammer holes that are the right size.
Beavers must measure and calculate to build their dams.

Mr. Badger O' Badge helps his students see how math
is hidden everywhere in the woods. In fact, he's in the middle
of a math lesson right now.
Let's take a look!

THE CLASSROOM IS ESPECIALLY QUIET TODAY AS THE STUDENTS WORK OUT SOME TRICKY PROBLEMS. **CAN YOU HELP THE ANIMALS COMPLETE THEIR WORK?**

AN ABACUS CAN HELP YOU ADD AND SUBTRACT MORE QUICKLY. FOLLOW THE DIRECTIONS TO BUILD YOUR OWN!

WHAT YOU NEED:
- A THICK PIECE OF CARDBOARD
- 10 BEADS OR TUBE-SHAPED PASTA PIECES
- STRING
- TAPE
- SHARP SCISSORS

1. Cut the cardboard into a rectangle about 5 inches long and 2 inches wide.
2. Punch a hole about 1/2 inch from the short edge. Do the same on the other side.
3. Insert the string into one of the holes and secure the end with tape on the back.
4. Slide 10 beads onto the string.
5. Insert the loose end to the other hole and secure with tape on the back.

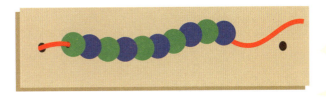

6. You're done! Now you can slide the beads across the string to help you add and subtract.

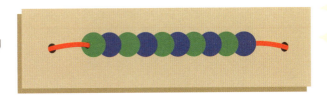

LET'S WARM UP WITH SOME ADDITION.

ADD THE NUMBERS AND **WRITE THE TOTAL FOR EACH PROBLEM**.

3+4=	4+5=	1+2+3=
9+1=	0+6=	5+3+2=
5+3=	4+4=	1+4+3=
2+2=	1+4=	8+1+1=

HERE WE GO!
COMPLETE EACH EQUATION.
THEN DRAW A LINE TO MATCH THE
EQUATIONS WITH THE SAME VALUE.

3+3=

2+6+1=

1+2=

3+1+1=

4+5=

3+1+2=

4+1=

0+2+1=

ADD CAREFULLY AS YOU
FOLLOW THE ARROWS.
WRITE THE FINAL NUMBER
AT THE END OF THE CHAIN.

THE LAST BELL OF THE DAY HAS RUNG.
SCHOOL IS OVER, BUT THE ROOM IS A MESS!
THE CLASS MUST TIDY UP BEFORE
GOING HOME. THESE BOOKS
BELONG IN BACKPACKS.

DRAW A LINE TO MATCH
EACH BOOK WITH A BACKPACK.
THE TWO NUMBERS WILL
ADD UP TO 10.

PUT YOUR CRAYONS AWAY;
EACH BOX MUST HAVE
10 CRAYONS TOTAL.

DRAW THE MISSING CRAYONS
IN EACH BOX. THEN FILL IN THE MISSING
NUMBER BELOW. USE THE CRAYON
SET AT THE TOP IF YOU NEED HELP.

$$7 + \boxed{} = 10$$

$$9 + \boxed{} = 10$$

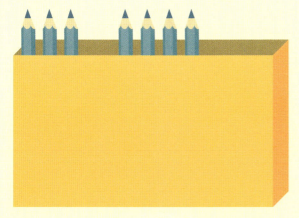

$$3 + 4 + \boxed{} = 10$$

$$5 + 1 + \boxed{} = 10$$

FOR EACH ROW, COLOR
THE LARGEST VALUE
RED AND **THE SMALLEST**
VALUE GREEN.

9   5   7   2   4

2   6   1   7   0

1+1   2+1   3+5   7+3   0+5

APPLES, PENCILS, TACKS, MARBLES, AND BOOKS—EVERYTHING MUST BE COUNTED! **WRITE THE NUMBER** FOR EACH ITEM, THEN FOLLOW THE DIRECTIONS AND **COLOR**.

COLOR THE BASKET
WITH FEWER APPLES.

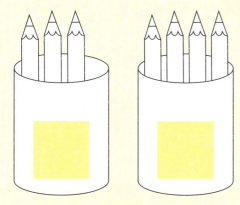

COLOR THE CAN
WITH FEWER PENCILS.

COLOR THE JARS
WITH THE SAME NUMBER OF THUMBTACKS.

COLOR THE BAG
WITH MORE MARBLES.

COLOR THE SHELF
WITH MORE BOOKS.

THE PASTRY SHOP

A delicious smell drifts though the woods.

All of Woodland Town knows exactly where the sweet smell comes from:
MR. AND MRS. RABBIT'S PASTRY SHOP.

Creatures from every corner of the woods come here to satisfy their sweet
cravings. Animals from the mountains make the long trek just for a taste,
and passing birds swoop down to sample the desserts.
During tea time, the shop overflows with cakes and cookies.

Mr. Rabbit's great-great grandparents opened the shop years ago.
The Rabbit family guards the large book of SECRET RECIPES.

The recipes are written in code so that nosy animals can't copy them.
Here is one of the codes. My Rabbit shared it with me only because
I helped him find a RARE INGREDIENT in the woods.

The name of the recipe is in a code.
CAN YOU HELP ME DECODE IT?

2	38	4	19	14	16	35	41	1
A	I	L	T	N	U	P	E	W

1								
W								

ORDER THE NUMBERS
FROM SMALLEST TO LARGEST AND WRITE
THE CORRESPONDING LETTERS.
THE NAME OF THE TREAT
WILL BE REVEALED!

20

NOW WE KNOW WHAT WE ARE BAKING.
BUT WE DON'T KNOW HOW TO BAKE IT!
HELP ME ADD THE NUMBERS. WRITE THE TOTAL
IN EACH BOX NEXT TO THE INGREDIENT.

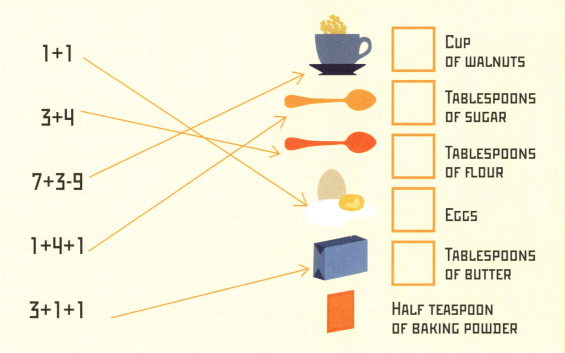

1+1

3+4

7+3-9

1+4+1

3+1+1

Cup
OF WALNUTS

TABLESPOONS
OF SUGAR

TABLESPOONS
OF FLOUR

Eggs

TABLESPOONS
OF BUTTER

HALF TEASPOON
OF BAKING POWDER

THANKS TO YOU, WE KNOW HOW MUCH
TO USE OF EACH INGREDIENT.
WE CAN FINALLY BAKE OUR TREAT.

WE DESERVE IT!

DIRECTIONS:

1. Separate the egg whites and yolks.
2. Beat the egg yolks, sugar,
and melted butter in a bowl.
2. Mix in the flour and baking
powder.
3. In a separate bowl, beat
the egg whites until stiff.
4. Chop the nuts. Add the egg
whites and chopped nuts to
the batter.
5. Pour the batter into a pie dish
and bake at 350 degrees for
30 minutes.

TODAY, MR. AND MRS. RABBIT ARE BUSY AT THE PASTRY SHOP. A BIG ORDER HAS BEEN PLACED FOR SQUIRREL'S BIRTHDAY PARTY.

Mr. Rabbit baked 3 SHEETS OF COOKIES. He placed 10 COOKIES on each sheet. While he was making the icing, the littlest rabbit in the family ate 4 cookies!

HOW MANY COOKIES WILL MR. RABBIT FIND WHEN HE RETURNS TO DECORATE THEM?

FINISH THE DRAWING AND FIGURE OUT HOW MANY COOKIES ARE LEFT.

There is no time to worry about the missing cookies.
Squirrel also ordered 4 JAM TARTS!

To bake 1 jam tart you need:
3 eggs
1 jar of jam
1 bag of flour

THE RABBITS ARE CHECKING THE PANTRY.
DO THEY HAVE ENOUGH OF EACH INGREDIENT
TO BAKE ALL 4 JAM TARTS? HELP COMPLETE THE
SHOPPING LIST WITH THE MISSING ITEMS.

THE GENERAL STORE

The General Store fills the hollow tree trunk of an old pine tree.
This cozy store has pencils, tools, needles, clocks, and anything else the
creatures of Woodland Town might need.
It's the end of the summer, so the shop is especially full
as the animals stock up for the cold season.

Mr. Hedgehog runs the General Store. He is prickly and precise.
Even when the shop is packed, he keeps everything in perfect order.
His motto is, "A place for everything and everything in its place."

MR. HEDGEHOG KEEPS TRACK OF EVERY ITEM IN THE STORE
BETTER THAN A COMPUTER CAN.
HE USES A NUMBER AND LETTER TO SHOW
THE EXACT LOCATION OF EACH ITEM IN
THE SHOP WINDOW.

FIND THE STICKERS AT THE END OF THE BOOK.
THEN USE THE NUMBER AND LETTER PAIRS
TO HELP MR. HEDGEHOG FINISH PLACING ITEMS
IN THE SHOP WINDOW.

- A MAGNIFYING
  GLASS:
  SPOT B2

- A TEAPOT:
  SPOT E6

- A HAMMER:
  SPOT H3

- A BUTTON:
  SPOT D8

- A PAIR OF SCISSORS:
  SPOT G5

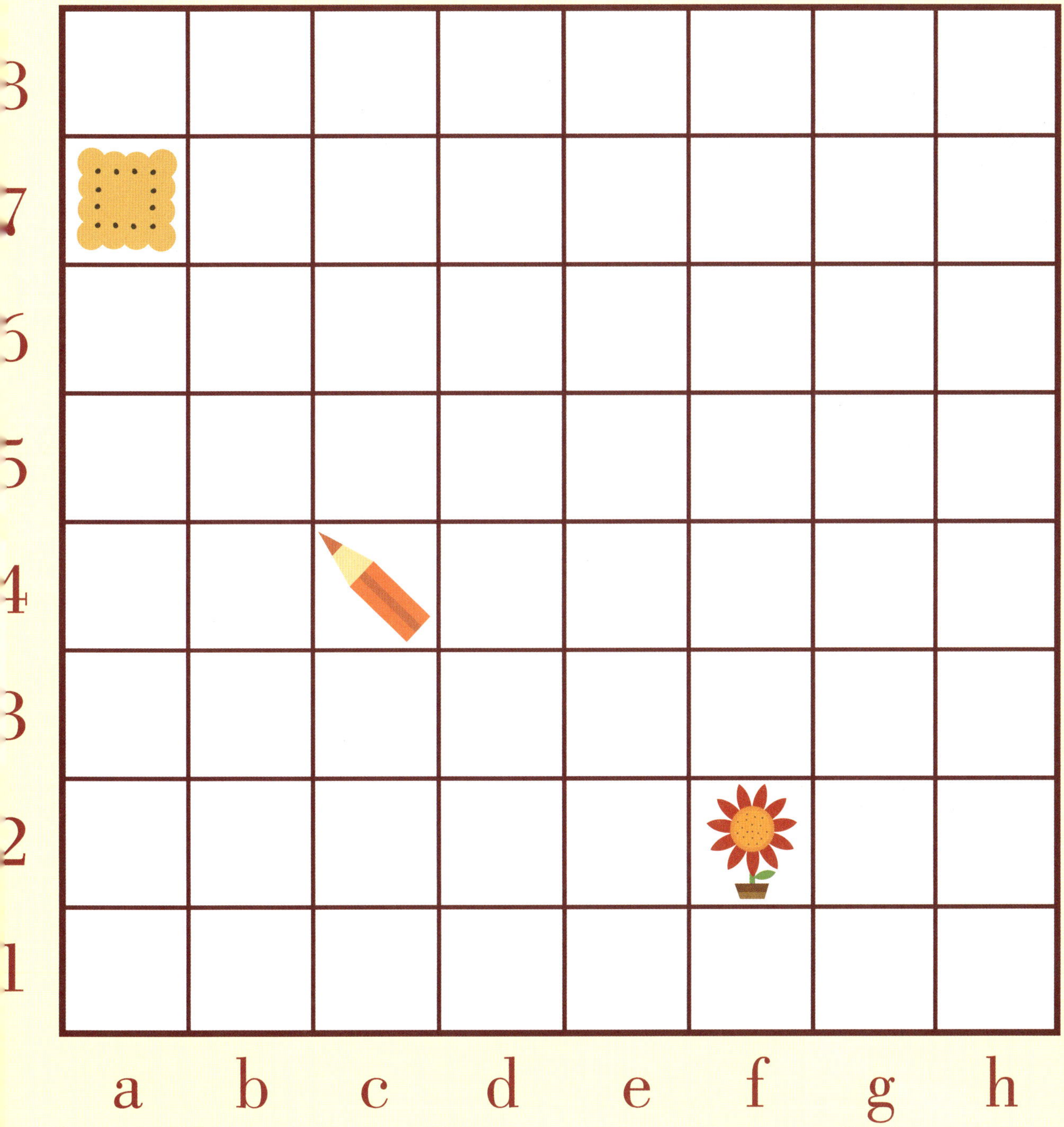

WRITE THE NUMBER AND
LETTER TO SHOW THE
LOCATION OF THESE ITEMS:

A PENCIL: SPOT _____

A FLOWER POT: SPOT _____

A COOKIE: SPOT _____

OH, NO! A GUST OF WIND BLEW AWAY ALL THE PRICE TAGS.
READ THE CLUES ON THE NEXT PAGE TO FIGURE
OUT THE CORRECT PRICES. THEN USE THE STICKERS
TO HELP MR. HEDGEHOG REPLACE THE PRICE TAGS.

*MAKE SURE YOU GET THE RIGHT PRICES! YOU WILL USE
THESE PRICES AGAIN ON THE PAGES THAT FOLLOW.*

FOLLOW THESE CLUES.

CHESTNUTS HAVE THE LOWEST PRICE

1 JAR OF HONEY COSTS THE SAME AS 3 PENCILS.

A JAR OF JAM COSTS LESS THAN A JAR OF NAILS.

IT IS VERY BUSY AT THE GENERAL STORE TODAY.
MANY ANIMALS HAVE PLACED ORDERS TO PREPARE
FOR WINTER AND HIBERNATION.

MR. HEDGEHOG HAS GATHERED
THE ITEMS FOR EACH ORDER.
USE THE PRICES FROM THE PREVIOUS PAGE
TO HELP HIM ADD UP THE TOTALS.

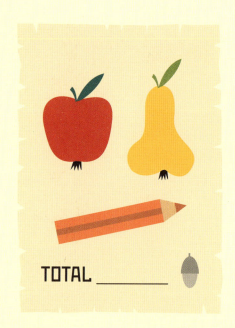

TOTAL _____

TOTAL _____

TOTAL _____

TOTAL _____

TOTAL _____

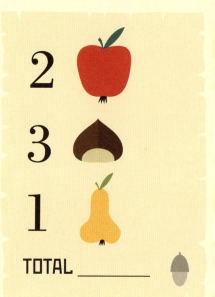

TOTAL _____

NICE WORK! TO THANK YOU FOR HELPING OUT ON THIS BUSY DAY, MR. HEDGEHOG HAS GIVEN YOU THESE COINS. ADD UP THE TOTAL AND DECIDE WHAT TO BUY AT THE GENERAL STORE. REFER TO THE PRICES FROM THE PREVIOUS PAGE. **DRAW OR WRITE** WHAT YOU WOULD LIKE TO BUY. DID YOU SPEND ALL THE MONEY?

IT'S ALMOST CLOSING TIME, BUT CUSTOMERS
ARE STILL COMING INTO THE STORE.
WHAT A BUSY DAY! REFER TO THE PRICES ON
THE PREVIOUS PAGE TO ANSWER THEIR QUESTIONS.

IS THIS MONEY ENOUGH TO BUY AN APPLE,
A PENCIL, AND A CHESTNUT?

_____

HOW MUCH MONEY DO I HAVE LEFT OVER?

_____

HOW MANY JARS OF HONEY
CAN I BUY WITH THIS MONEY?

_____

WILL I HAVE ANY MONEY LEFT OVER?

_____

CUT OUT THIS PAGE AND GLUE IT ONTO A PIECE OF CARDBOARD. THEN **CUT OUT THE COINS AND TAGS**. PLAY WITH THEM AS YOU PRETEND TO BE A SHOPKEEPER OR A CUSTOMER. YOU CAN ALSO USE THE OTHER TAGS AND STICKERS FROM THE BOOK.

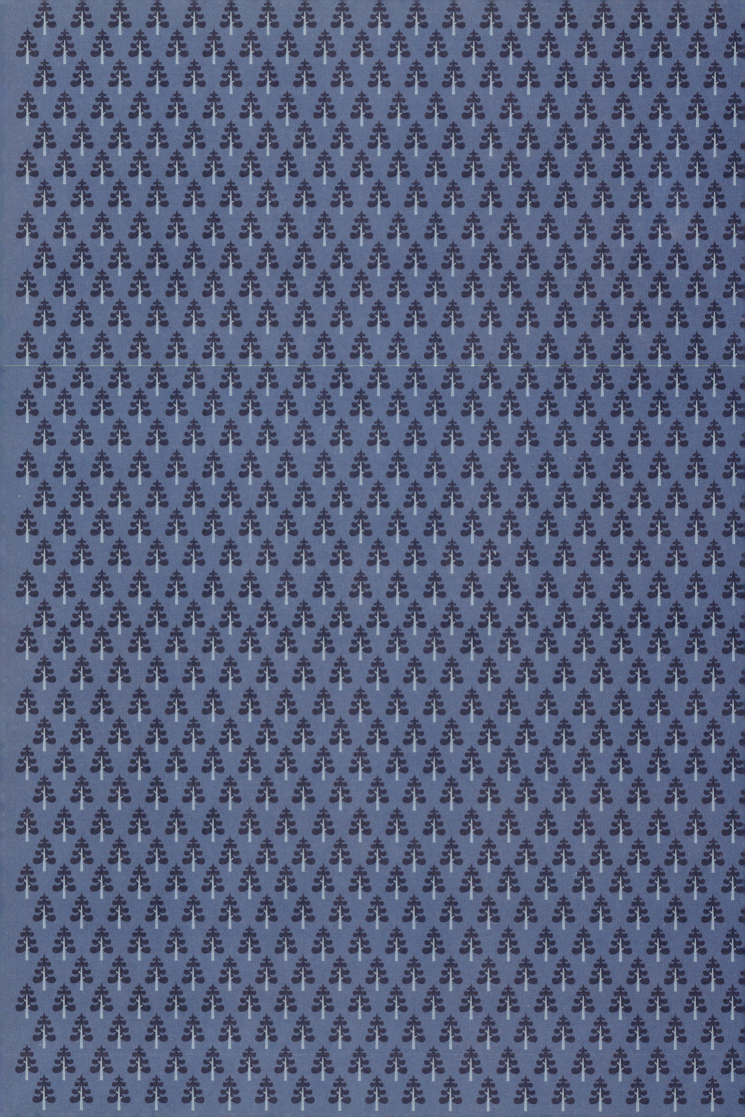

THERE IS NO TIME TO REST AT THE GENERAL
STORE. NEW ITEMS JUST ARRIVED! BEFORE
THE ITEMS CAN BE PLACED ON SHELVES,
MR. HEDGEHOG MUST FIGURE OUT
THE RIGHT PRICES.

$+$ $=$ 2

$+$ $=$ 4

$+$ $+$ $=$ 6

$+$ $+$ $=$

USE THE CLUES ABOVE TO FIGURE OUT THE
PRICE FOR EACH ITEM. WRITE THE **CORRECT
PRICES** IN THE BOXES BELOW.

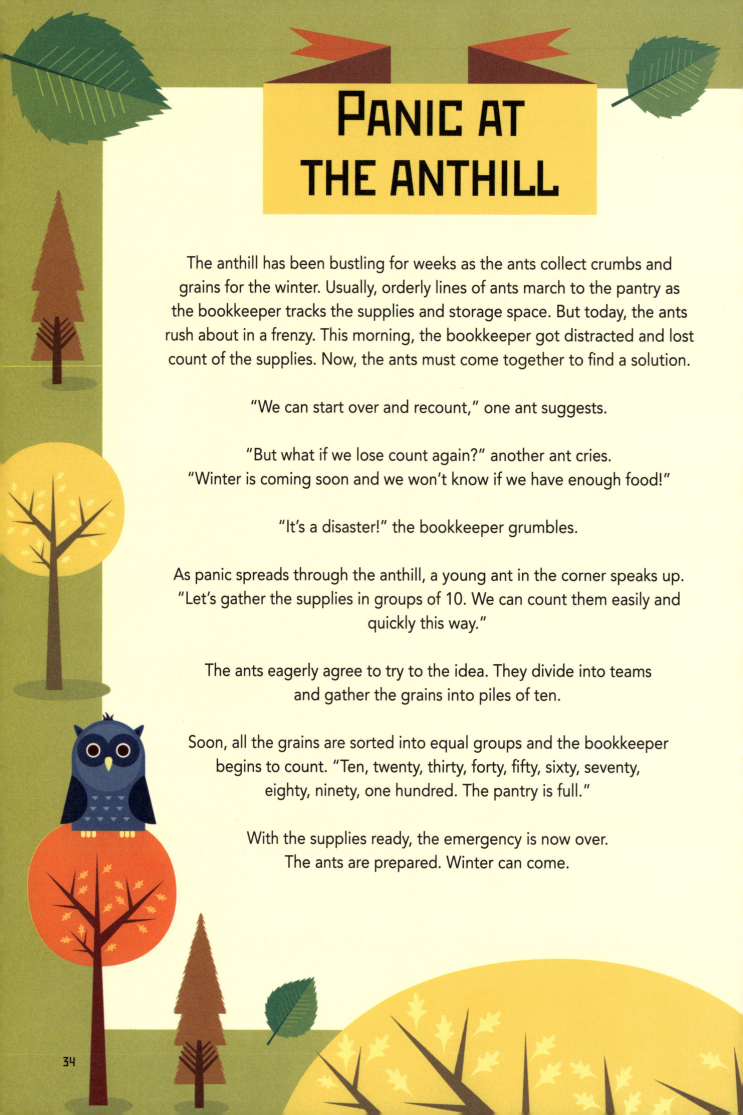

PANIC AT THE ANTHILL

The anthill has been bustling for weeks as the ants collect crumbs and grains for the winter. Usually, orderly lines of ants march to the pantry as the bookkeeper tracks the supplies and storage space. But today, the ants rush about in a frenzy. This morning, the bookkeeper got distracted and lost count of the supplies. Now, the ants must come together to find a solution.

"We can start over and recount," one ant suggests.

"But what if we lose count again?" another ant cries.
"Winter is coming soon and we won't know if we have enough food!"

"It's a disaster!" the bookkeeper grumbles.

As panic spreads through the anthill, a young ant in the corner speaks up. "Let's gather the supplies in groups of 10. We can count them easily and quickly this way."

The ants eagerly agree to try to the idea. They divide into teams and gather the grains into piles of ten.

Soon, all the grains are sorted into equal groups and the bookkeeper begins to count. "Ten, twenty, thirty, forty, fifty, sixty, seventy, eighty, ninety, one hundred. The pantry is full."

With the supplies ready, the emergency is now over.
The ants are prepared. Winter can come.

HELP! THERE ARE
SO MANY GRAINS
TO COUNT!

IF WE ORGANIZE THE GRAINS INTO ROWS OF TEN,
WE CAN COUNT THEM TEN AT A TIME. LET'S COUNT
THE GROUPS TOGETHER.

TEN, TWENTY, THIRTY, FORTY, FIFTY, SIXTY,
SEVENTY, EIGHTY, NINETY AND ONE HUNDRED!

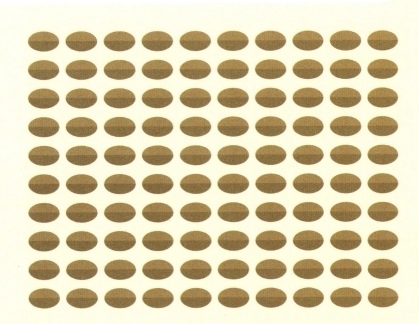

IT'S SIMPLE TO COUNT EVEN TINY GRAINS OF RICE WHEN THEY ARE PUT IN ORDER. WRITE THE CORRECT NUMBER ON EACH GRAIN AS YOU COUNT UP TO 100.

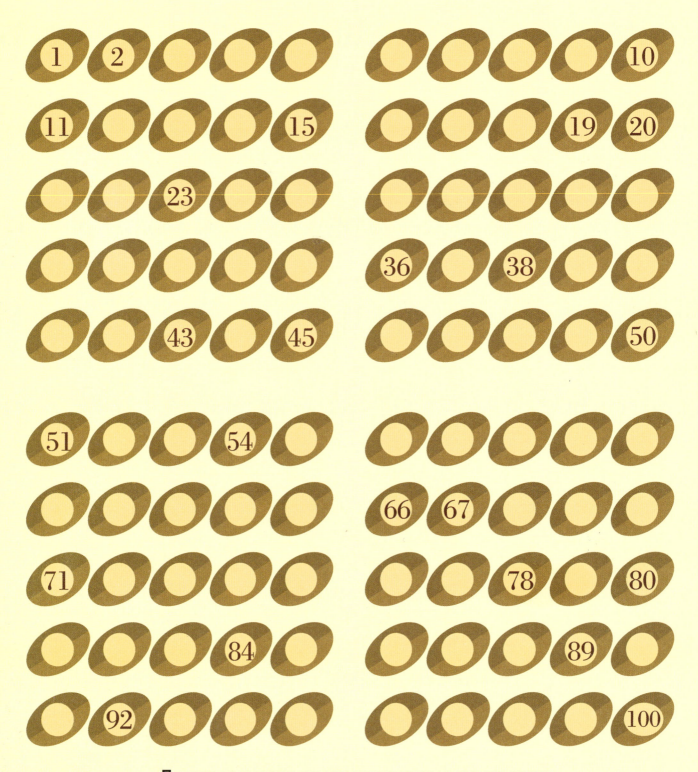

REPEAT EACH ROW OF NUMBERS FROM LEFT TO RIGHT
AND FROM RIGHT TO LEFT.
REPEAT EACH COLUMN OF NUMBERS FROM
TOP TO BOTTOM AND BOTTOM TO TOP.
THE MORE YOU PRACTICE, THE FASTER YOU
WILL BE ABLE TO COUNT!

EACH OF THE WAREHOUSES IN THE
ANTHILL HOLDS 50 GRAINS.
LET'S SEE HOW CLOSE THEY ARE
TO FILLING UP THE WAREHOUSES.

GRAINS COLLECTED ____
MISSING GRAINS ____

GRAINS COLLECTED ____
MISSING GRAINS ____

GRAINS COLLECTED ____
MISSING GRAINS ____

GRAINS COLLECTED ____
MISSING GRAINS ____

GRAINS COLLECTED ____
MISSING GRAINS ____

GRAINS COLLECTED ____
MISSING GRAINS ____

ALL THE ANIMALS IN WOODLAND TOWN MUST STORE FOOD FOR THE WINTER. FOLLOW THE DIRECTIONS AND **COMPLETE EACH DRAWING**. THEN **COUNT THE TOTAL AMOUNT EACH ANIMAL** WILL HAVE SAVED.

MR. HEDGEHOG HAS 3 CASES IN THE PANTRY. HE PUTS 5 APPLES IN EACH CASE.

HOW MANY APPLES WILL HE HAVE SAVED FOR THE LONG WINTER?

_____

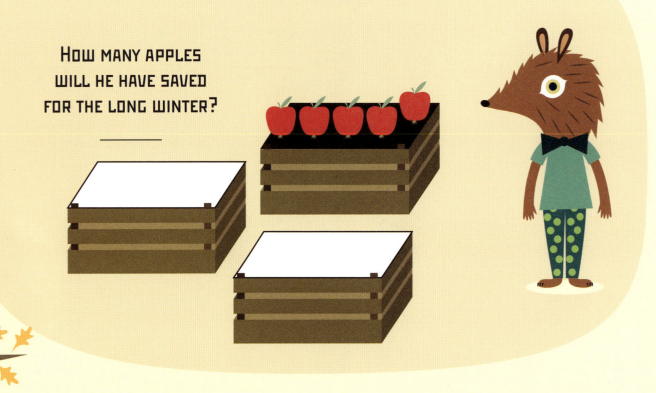

SQUIRREL FILLS 4 BOWLS WITH 6 HAZELNUTS IN EACH BOWL.

HOW MANY NUTS WILL HE HAVE DURING HIBERNATION?

_____

BEAR HAS A SWEET TOOTH, SO HE FILLS HIS SHELVES
WITH HONEY. EACH CABINET HAS 3 SHELVES.
HE PUTS 5 JARS OF HONEY ON EACH SHELF.

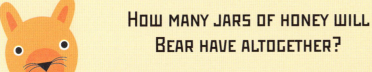

HOW MANY JARS OF HONEY WILL
BEAR HAVE ALTOGETHER?

_____

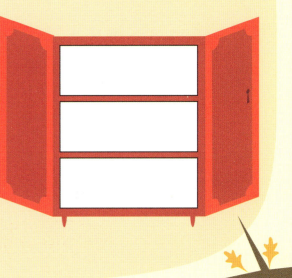

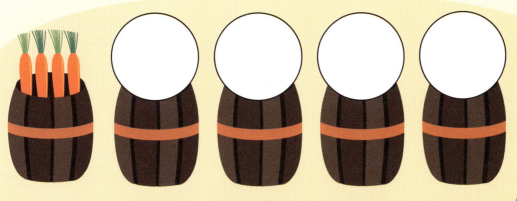

MR. RABBIT FILLS 5 BARRELS WITH 4 CARROTS
IN EACH BARREL. THE LITTLEST RABBIT EATS ONE
CARROT FROM THE FIRST BARREL AND TWO CARROTS
FROM THE SECOND BARREL.

HOW MANY CARROTS
ARE LEFT IN THE BARRELS
TO KEEP FOR WINTER?

_____

THE MICE TWINS, TIP AND TOP, NEED YOUR HELP!
THEY COLLECTED SUPPLIES ALL DAY AND EACH ONE
THINKS THAT HE HAS COLLECTED THE MOST. HELP THEM
SETTLE THEIR ARGUMENT BY COUNTING THE SUPPLIES.

TIP FILLED 2 BASKETS
WITH 6 RASPBERRIES
IN EACH BASKET.

BASKETS:____
RASPBERRIES IN EACH
BASKET:_____
RASPBERRIES IN TOTAL: _____

TOP PUT 3 RASPBERRIES
IN EACH CRATE.
HE HAD 3 CRATES.

CRATES:____
RASPBERRIES IN EACH
CRATE:_____
RASPBERRIES IN TOTAL: _____

TIP HARVESTED PLUMS.
HE PUT 2 PLUMS IN EACH
OF HIS 5 BAGS.

BAGS:____
PLUMS IN EACH BAG:_____
PLUMS IN TOTAL: _____

TOP FILLED 2 BOWLS
WITH 7 PLUMS IN
EACH BOWL.

BOWLS:____
PLUMS IN EACH BOWL:_____
PLUMS IN TOTAL: _____

TIP HAS COLLECTED 10 SMALL
GROUPS OF CHERRIES.
EACH GROUP HAS 2 CHERRIES.

GROUPS OF CHERRIES:____
CHERRIES IN EACH GROUP:_____
CHERRIES IN TOTAL: _____

TOP PICKED CHERRIES AND PUT
THEM IN 4 BASKETS. HE PUT 4
CHERRIES IN EACH BASKET.

BASKETS:____
CHERRIES IN EACH BASKET:_____
CHERRIES IN TOTAL: _____

TIP PUT 9 GRAINS OF WHEAT
INTO EACH BAG.
HE FILLED 4 BAGS.

BAGS:____
GRAINS IN EACH BAG:____
GRAINS IN TOTAL:____

TOP FILLED 7 JARS,
PUTTING 7 GRAINS
OF WHEAT IN EACH JAR.

JARS:____
GRAINS IN EACH JAR:____
GRAINS IN TOTAL:____

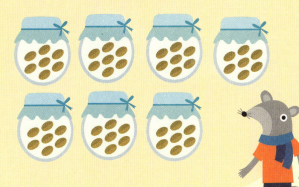

I HAVE COLLECTED MANY SUPPLIES
FOR THE WINTER TOO.
PLEASE HELP ME COUNT THEM!

How many
plums?

6+6+6+6=____

OR

6x4=____

TOTAL

How many
mushrooms?

7+7+7+7+7=____

OR

7x__=____

TOTAL

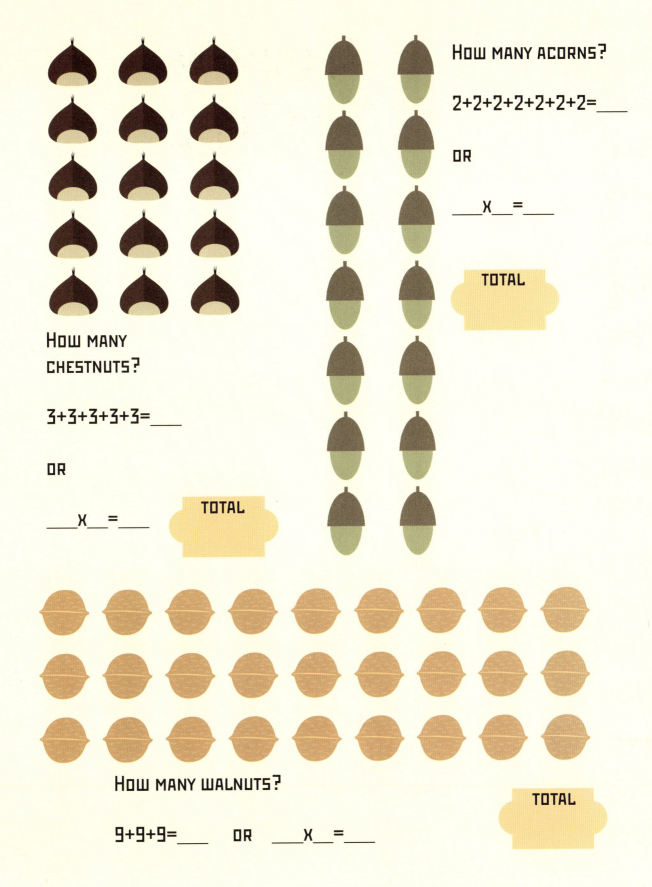

How many chestnuts?

3+3+3+3+3=____

OR

____X____=____

TOTAL

How many acorns?

2+2+2+2+2+2+2=____

OR

____X____=____

TOTAL

How many walnuts?

9+9+9=____   OR   ____X____=____

TOTAL

WHAT IS THE TOTAL NUMBER OF PLUMS, CHESTNUTS, ACORNS, MUSHROOMS, AND WALNUTS ALTOGETHER?

____+____+____+____+____=

TOTAL

A WINDY WARNING

Every year, fall fades to winter in the same way.
The sun fails to rise above the Great Oak.
A cool breeze begins to brush past the trees.
Nests gently rock, and leaves tumble from branches.
The North Wind warns Woodland Town that winter is nearly here.

The animals must act quickly. There is much to do.
They prepare their dens and nests. Some repair holes
to keep out the cold. Others gather straw to make beds
for the long winter nap. And of course, all the animals
must fill their pantries!
Grains, seeds, grass, and berries can't
be scavenged in the winter.

Today, the change begins. The sun could not rise above the Great Oak,
so the village remains in shadows. Animals sniff the air,
their noses tingling as they await the wind.
The wind creates chaos in Woodland Town,
and the animals must be ready.

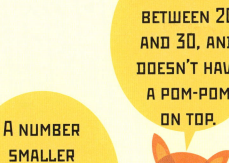

A NUMBER SMALLER THAN 20 IS ON MY HAT.

MY HAT HAS A NUMBER BETWEEN 20 AND 30, AND DOESN'T HAVE A POM-POM ON TOP.

MY HAT HAS A POM-POM ON TOP. IT DOES *NOT* HAVE THE HIGHEST NUMBER.

ADD 10 TO THE FOX'S HAT TO FIND MY HAT.

ON MY HAT THERE IS A NUMBER BETWEEN 30 AND 32.

WHAT A MESS! MRS. HEDGEHOG HAD
JUST HUNG THE LAST PIECE OF LAUNDRY
WHEN THE WIND SCATTERED EVERYTHING
ON THE GROUND. USE THE STICKERS
AND HELP MRS. HEDGEHOG HANG
THE CLOTHES ON THE CLOTHESLINE.
ARRANGE THEM IN ORDER
**FROM THE LOWEST
TO HIGHEST NUMBER.**

THE WIND CREATED A MESS AT MOUSE'S
MAGAZINE STAND TOO! SOLVE
THE EQUATION ON EACH MAGAZINE.
THEN USE THE STICKERS TO ARRANGE
THEM **FROM THE LARGEST
TO SMALLEST** VALUE.

45-5

30+16

30-10

12+10

18+5

22+13

FALL BRINGS SHORTER DAYS AND COOL WEATHER. THE LEAVES CHANGE COLOR AND BEGIN TO FALL.

SOLVE THE EQUATION INSIDE EACH LEAF. THEN **COLOR THE LEAVES** ACCORDING TO THE KEY ON THE LEFT.

34

32

25

28

20

10+22

17+15

12+8

17+3

20+14

45-20

22+12

40-12

35-15

21+4

40-6

20+12

18+10

15+13

11+23

15+10

9+11

30-5

50-30

40-8

38-4

35-3

13+12

19+9

38-10

THE WOODLAND TOWN GAMES

The woods hum with excitement today. The bumblebees hang banners.
The badgers tidy up the field. And the beavers are building benches.
Why? An audience will soon come to watch the Woodland Town Games!

Every year, the animals join together to celebrate the end of winter.
Woodland Town welcomes a new spring with a day of sunshine,
sports, and friends.

Woodpecker provides a steady beat as the crickets and cicadas play
an anthem to kick off the festivities. From sack races to the high jump,
there is a game to suit every animal. Frogs leap gracefully into the pond
for the diving competition. Squirrels pass nuts in the relay race.
The animals divide into two teams and hold on tight to a tree vine
in a giant tug-of-war game. By the end of the day, every animal
wears a medal.

When the games end, the party begins! Music, laughter,
and delicious treats from the pastry shop fill the forest.
The animals are tired, but happy, as they return to their homes,
ready to greet the spring.

WHAT IS THE MASCOT FOR WOODLAND
GAME DAY? SOLVE THE PROBLEM IN EACH
BOX AND THEN COLOR ACCORDING
TO THE KEY. WHEN ALL THE BOXES ARE
COLORED, YOU'LL SEE THE MASCOT!

10	→	RED			
30	→	LIGHT BROWN			
40	→	DARK BROWN			
50	→	GREEN			

30+20							
40+10	25+25						

			0+40				
	43-3	31+9	36+4	48-8	10+30		
	50-10	28+12	40+0	25+15	1+39	40-0	29+11
33+7	49-9	30+10	39+1	20+20	34+6	35+5	32+8	45-5
	30+0	25+5	50-20	10+20	5+25	19+11	1+29
	2+28		16+14	28+2	35-5		24+6
	41-11	15+15	36-6	6+4	30-0	14+16	32-2
	12+18	40-10	21+9	20+10	29+1	22+8	17+13
		23+7	18+12	23+7	26+4	19+11	
			7+23	11+19	3+27		

THE ARCHERY COMPETITION
IS UNDERWAY!

EACH PLAYER SHOT **FOUR ARROWS**
INTO THE TARGET. ADD UP THE TOTAL
POINTS TO FIGURE OUT WHO WON
EACH MATCH.

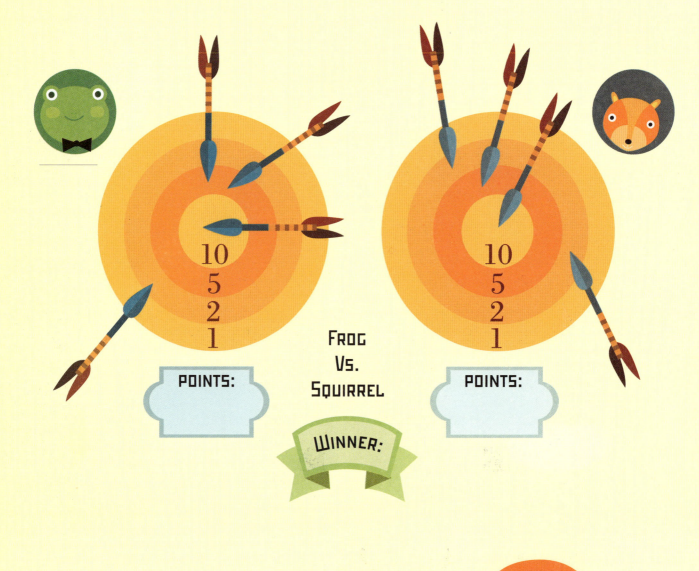

FROG
VS.
SQUIRREL

POINTS:

POINTS:

WINNER:

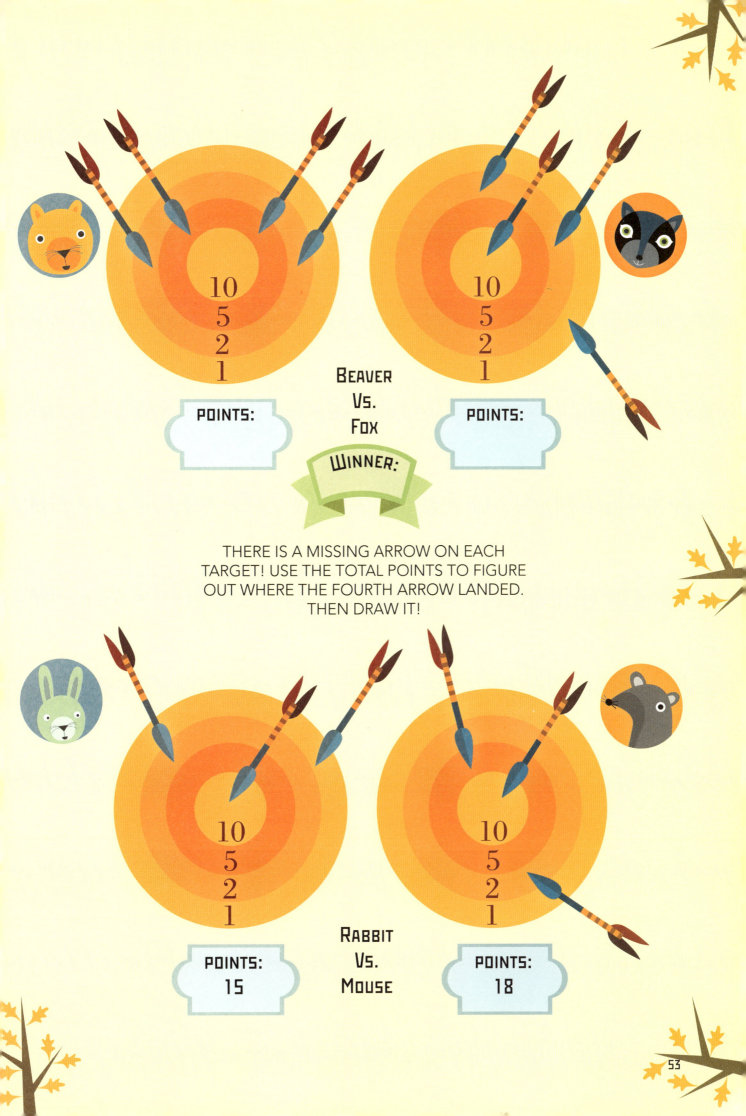

BEAVER
VS.
FOX

POINTS:

POINTS:

WINNER:

THERE IS A MISSING ARROW ON EACH
TARGET! USE THE TOTAL POINTS TO FIGURE
OUT WHERE THE FOURTH ARROW LANDED.
THEN DRAW IT!

RABBIT
VS.
MOUSE

POINTS:
15

POINTS:
18

FROG, GRASSHOPPER, CRICKET, AND MOUSE COMPETE IN THE JUMPING CONTEST. EACH HAS A STRATEGY. SOME TAKE A FEW LONG JUMPS, AND OTHERS TAKE MANY SHORT JUMPS.

ADD AS YOU GO TO FILL IN THE MISSING NUMBERS ALONG EACH PATH. WRITE THE TOTAL POINTS FOR EACH ANIMAL. WHO WON THE CONTEST?

EVERY LEAP IS WORTH 5

0   5

EVERY LEAP IS WORTH 4

0   4

EVERY LEAP IS WORTH 3

0   3

0   EVERY LEAP IS WORTH 7   7

TOTAL:

TOTAL:

TOTAL:

TOTAL:

WHICH ANIMAL PLACED FIRST, SECOND, THIRD, AND FOURTH? PUT EACH ANIMAL'S STICKER ON THE CORRECT PODIUM STEP.

1

2

3

4

55

Did you get all the answers right?

Find out in the ANSWER KEY!

8   7   0   1
4   9   3
6   2
5

9
8
10
7
5

six   five   three   seven   eight   3   4   two   0   2   1   9   7   zero   6   5   8   four   nine   one

HOW MANY PIECES OF GREEN FRUIT ARE THERE ALTOGETHER? 3

HOW MANY FRUITS HAVE THEY COLLECTED ALTOGETHER?16

HOW MANY PIECES OF FRUIT ARE NOT YELLOW? 8

THE ORANGE-SHELLED SNAIL HAS COLLECTED MORE FRUIT THAN THE OTHERS

3+4=7   4+5=9   1+2+3=6

9+1=10   0+6=6   5+3+2=10

5+3=8   4+4=8   1+4+3=8

2+2=4   1+4=5   8+1+1=10

3+3=6   2+6+1=9

1+2=3   3+1+1=5

4+5=9   3+1+2=6

4+1=5   0+2+1=3

+3   +1   +2   +2   +1
3   6   7   9   1   10

+3   +2   +1   +1   +3
0   3   9   10   4   7

$7 + \boxed{3} = 10$ $9 + \boxed{1} = 10$

$3 + 4 + \boxed{3} = 10$ $5 + 1 + \boxed{4} = 10$

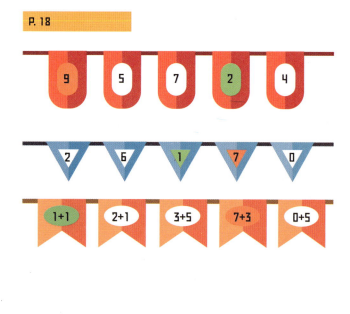

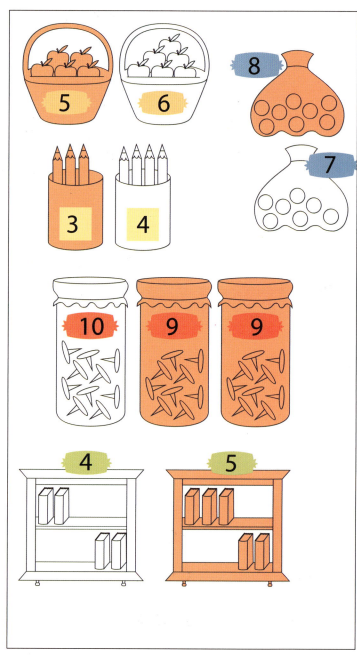

2	38	4	19	14	16	35	41	1
A	I	L	T	N	U	P	E	Ш

1	2	4	14	16	19		35	38	41
Ш	A	L	N	U	T		P	I	E

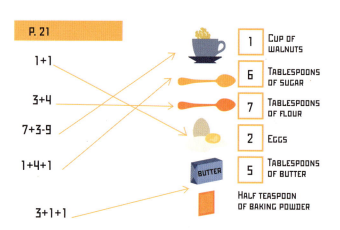

1+1

3+4

7+3-9

1+4+1

3+1+1

1	Cup of walnuts
6	Tablespoons of sugar
7	Tablespoons of flour
2	Eggs
5	Tablespoons of butter
	Half teaspoon of baking powder

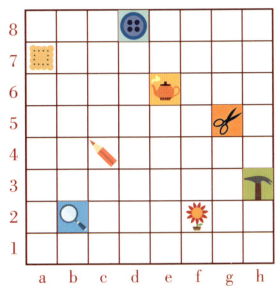

A PENCIL: SPOT C4
A FLOWER POT: SPOT F2
A COOKIE: SPOT A7

Total: 9

Total: 13

Total: 18

Total: 18

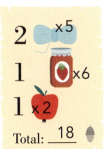

Total: 18

Total: 11

IS THIS MONEY ENOUGH TO BUY
AN APPLE, A PENCIL AND A CHESTNUT?
2+3+1= 8 COINS
HOW MUCH MONEY
DO I HAVE LEFT OVER?
2 COINS

HOW MANY JARS OF HONEY
CAN I BUY WITH THIS MONEY?
18 COINS, 2 JARS
WILL I HAVE ANY MONEY LEFT OVER?
NO

P. 33

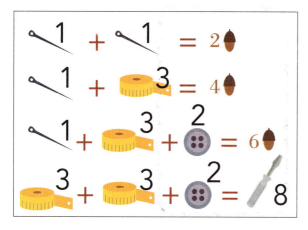

P. 36

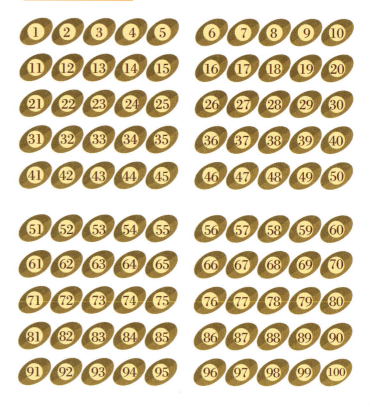

P. 37

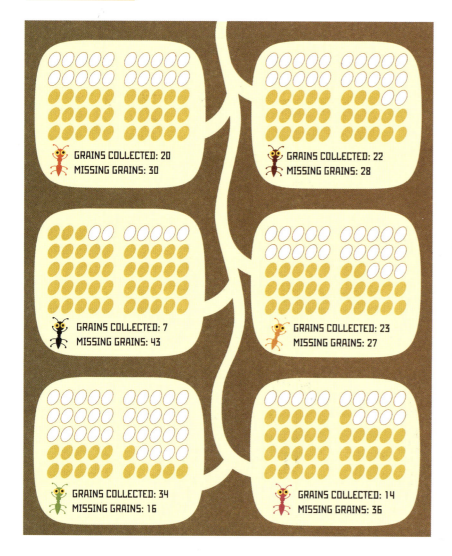

PP. 38-39

MR. HEDGEHOG WILL HAVE SAVED 15 APPLES.

THE SQUIRREL WILL HAVE 24 NUTS.

THE BEAR HAS IN THE PANTRY 30 JARS OF HONEY.

AT THE END THE HARES WILL HAVE IN THE PANTRY 17 CARROTS.

BASKETS: 2
RASPBERRIES IN EACH BASKET: 6
RASPBERRIES IN TOTAL: 12

BOXES: 2
PLUMS IN EACH BOX: 7
PLUMS IN TOTAL: 14

BAGS: 5
GRAINS IN EACH BAG: 9
GRAINS IN TOTAL: 45

CRATES: 3
RASPBERRIES IN EACH CRATE: 3
RASPBERRIES IN TOTAL: 9

SMALL GROUPS: 10
CHERRIES IN EACH SMALL GROUP: 2
CHERRIES IN TOTAL: 20

JARS: 7
GRAINS IN EACH JAR: 7
GRAINS IN TOTAL: 49

BAGS: 5
PLUMS IN EACH BAG: 2
PLUMS IN TOTAL: 10

BASKETS: 4
CHERRIES IN EACH BASKET: 4
CHERRIES IN TOTAL: 16

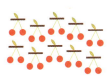

HOW MANY PLUMS?
6+6+6+6=24
OR
6X4=24

HOW MANY CHESTNUTS?
3+3+3+3+3=15
OR
3 X 5 =15

HOW MANY ACORNS?
2+2+2+2+2+2+2=14
OR
2 X 7 =14

HOW MANY MUSHROOMS?
7+7+7+7+7= 35
OR
7X5 =35

HOW MANY WALNUTS?
9+9+9=27
OR   9 X3 = 27

HOW MANY SUPPLIES ARE THERE
IN TOTAL IN MY PANTRY?
24 + 35 + 14 + 15 + 27 =

TOTAL
115

 17
 24
 34
 26
 31

19   23   27   38   41   44

30+16   45-5   22+13   18+5   12+10   30-10

Points 22 Points 19

Wins

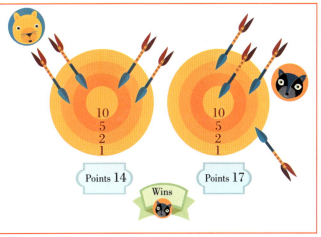

Points 14 Points 17

Wins

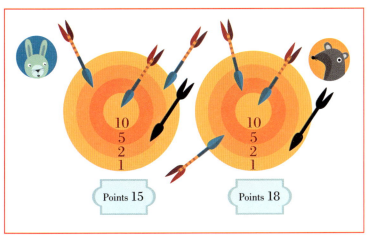

Points 15 Points 18

LINDA BERTOLA

Linda Bertola graduated from the Università Cattolica of Milan with a degree in Language Mediation and Intercultural Communication. She works both in and out the classroom to support students with learning differences and special needs. She also specializes in teaching Italian to foreign language learners of all ages. As an intercultural educator and trainer, Linda brings her expertise to a variety of schools and organizations. She shares her passion for the science of teaching, mathematics, and logic games with those she works with as well as on her website, genitoricrescono.com.

AGNESE BARUZZI

Agnese Baruzzi graduated in Graphic Design from ISIA (Higher Institute for Artistic Industries) of Urbino. Since 2001, she has worked as an illustrator, contributing to books for children in in Italy, the U.K., Japan, Portugal, the U.S., France, and Korea. She holds workshops for children and adults in schools and libraries. She also collaborates with many agencies, design studios, and publishers. Her enthusiasm and creativity shine through in the many books she has illustrated for White Star Kids.

New York

FLASH KIDS and the distinctive Flash Kids logo are registered trademarks of Barnes and Noble, Inc.

© 2017 White Star s.r.l.

First Flash Kids edition published in 2018.

ISBN 978-1-4114-7906-7

Distributed in Canada by Sterling Publishing
c/o Canadian Manda Group, 664 Annette Street
Toronto, Ontario, M6S 2C8, Canada

For information about custom editions, special sales, and premium and corporate purchases, please contact Sterling Special Sales at 800-805-5489 or specialsales@sterlingpublishing.com.

Manufactured in China
Lot #:
2 4 6 8 10 9 7 5 3 1
01/18

flashkids.com

Translation: Iceigeo, Milan (Renata Grilli, James Schwarten)

THE GENERAL STORE

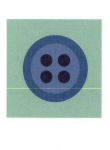

A WINDY WARNING

THE WOODLAND TOWN GAMES

COINS AND TAGS

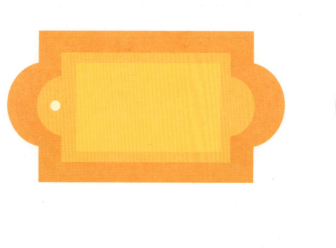
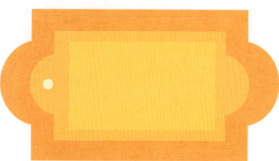

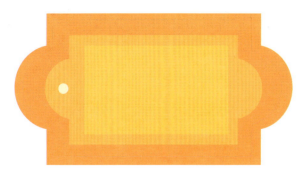

THE
MEDALS